Sandra De Souza is an Associate Solicitor specialising in complex medical negligence claims. Sandra has particular expertise in amputation; spinal injury/cauda equina; adult brain injury and child birth injury cases. She is recognised by her clients for her meticulous approach, commitment, and compassion.

Manpreet Singh is an Associate Solicitor at Irwin Mitchell practising in medical negligence. With almost 10 years post qualification experience, Manpreet acts for claimants in complex cases involving serious and catastrophic injuries arising from medical negligence, and has experience of acting in amputation claims. Manpreet has presented on the assessment of damages in amputation cases.

A Practical Guide to Clinical Negligence and Personal Injury Amputation Claims

A Practical Guide to Clinical Negligence and Personal Injury Amputation Claims

Sandra De Souza, Associate Solicitor
Manpreet Singh, Associate Solicitor

Law Brief Publishing

Published 2026 by Law Brief Publishing, an imprint of Law Brief Publishing Ltd
30 The Parks
Minehead
Somerset
TA24 8BT

www.lawbriefpublishing.com

Paperback: 978-1-918241-10-5

With thanks to our families – especially Florence and Elsie

PREFACE

'A Practical Guide to Clinical Negligence and Personal Injury Amputation Claims' is a handbook for legal practitioners handling complex, high value areas of litigation. Combining legal expertise with practical insight, this guide will help readers understand the medical causes and complications of limb loss - navigating expert evidence, rehabilitation pathways, and quantum assessment.

Authored by experienced practitioners, the book explains the medico-legal issues that regularly arise in amputation litigation. Readers are guided through best practices in instructing experts, avoiding evidential pitfalls and valuing prosthetic claims.

Comprehensive and accessible, this book is a great reference for claimant and defendant practitioners alike.

The law quoted is believed to be correct at 16th December 2025.

Sandra De Souza
Manpreet Singh
February 2026

CONTENTS

CHAPTER ONE

AMPUTATION CLAIMS: INSTANCES WHICH CAN CAUSE AMPUTATIONS

Potential claims which can give rise to amputations

There are a number of potential claims that can give rise to amputations, both from a personal injury and clinical negligence perspective. Establishing liability in personal injury claims can be more straightforward; claims most commonly arise from a road traffic accident or accidents at work. However, in clinical negligence cases establishing a causal link between negligent treatment and amputation injury can be complex.

Vascular surgery

A significant proportion of amputations in the UK are caused by nerve damage, circulatory problems, vascular conditions or delay in diagnosis of an infection. There is an unusually large number of clinical negligence claims arising from vascular surgery.

In 2021, an observational study[1] was undertaken into the trends of clinical negligence claims in vascular surgery within the United Kingdom. The study found 1,189 vascular surgery claims over the 13 years, showing a consistent upward trajectory that is expected to continue.

Treatment delays were the leading cause of clinical negligence claims in vascular surgery, while lower-limb amputation was the most frequently reported primary injury.

The study concluded that improved communication with patients and a higher surgical skill level could significantly reduce future claims.

Diabetes

Claims can often arise from mismanagement of patients with diabetes. In 2022 a study was undertaken into clinical negligence claims arising from diabetes and lower limb complications. The study identified the following:

- Failures to identify those patients that were high-risk and as such, those patients received minimal preventative care.
- Delays in and/or a failure to identify the extent and severity of pathology.
- Delays in the patient being seen by a specialist footcare team once a diagnosis was made.
- The assessments and treatments fell short of being evidence-based and care was unable to stop progression of the disease. Most patients were under a clinical team but outpatient interventions didn't stop the need for emergency medicine or inpatient input.
- Lack of effective or standardised processes for admitting patients to hospital. Incomplete assessments, imprecise notes that didn't have a clear meaning were also observed.

- Severe delays from the initial vascular assessment to the point of revascularisation.

- Imaging performed late in the progression of the pathology and poorly correlated to the clinical picture

- High levels of non-compliance but there was evidence of emotional and social factors and limited evidence of diabetic lower limb education provided.

The above are instances that could give rise to potential negligence cases resulting in amputation injury. In addition to these, there should always be careful consideration of management post-surgery and whether the patient has suffered any complications.

Complications following an amputation

Age, type of amputation and general health can all influence the risk of complications arising from an amputation. The risk of complication is lower in planned amputations than emergency ones. The following are common complications which may arise:

- Oedema of the residual limb may result in wound breakdown, pain, reduced mobility and difficulties with fitting a prosthetic.

- Wound infection can increase morbidity and have a negative effect on healing, phantom pain and the time to prosthetic fitting. Risk factors for infection can be diabetes, old age and smoking.

- Tissue necrosis

- Balance and stability issues due to loss of natural ankle

- Hair follicle infections
- Skin blisters
- Muscle contractures
- The spine may be affected because of altered gate and autonomic dysfunction.
- Osteomyelitis can sometimes be masked by deep and infected sinus.
- Pain including post-amputation pain, residual pain and phantom limb sensation.

Where a Claimant has suffered any of the above complications, consideration must be given to these and whether they have occurred as a result of negligence. For example, where wound breakdown or infection has occurred the post-surgical management should be investigated including whether regular wound inspection has occurred.

In addition to complications, co-existing pathology should be considered such as vascular pain, musculoskeletal pain and neuromas. There might also be prosthetic pain.

It's important to consider complications and the effects of the same on a Claimant's rehabilitation and/or use of their prosthetic. For example, there will be a period of time where a prosthetic cannot be used which in turn will impact on the Claimant's care needs, their ability to work and accommodation requirements. Practitioners also need to have an awareness of and understand the treatments which are available and may assist in improving the condition.

References

1. Hansrani, V. et al. Published in Annals of Vascular Surgery, vol 70, Jan 2021 https://pubmed.ncbi.nlm.nih.gov/32946996/

2. NHS Resolution (2022) *Diabetes and lower limb complications: A thematic review of clinical negligence claims*. NHS Resolution. Available at: https://resolution.nhs.uk/wp-content/uploads/2022/06/Diabetes_and_Lower_Limb_Complications.pdf

3. StatPearls (n.d.) *Lower Extremity Amputation*. In: *StatPearls* [Internet]. NCBI Bookshelf. Available at: https://www.ncbi.nlm.nih.gov/books/NBK546594/

4. Physiopedia (n.d.) *Complications Post Amputation*. Physiopedia. Available at: https://www.physio-pedia.com/Complications_Post_Amputation

5. NHS (n.d.) *Amputation*. NHS. Available at: https://www.nhs.uk/conditions/amputation/

CHAPTER TWO

EXPERT SPECIALISMS TO CONSIDER FOR INSTRUCTION

Expert's overriding duty to the Court

Civil Procedure Rule (CPR) 35.3 sets out that the expert's duty is to help the Court on matters within their expertise and this duty overrides any obligation to the instructing or paying party.

In determining whether a party should have permission to rely on an expert, the Court will consider whether that evidence is reasonably required to resolve the proceedings (CPR 35.1). Therefore, practitioners must carefully consider the expert specialisms for instruction.

Claimant practitioners should speak with their client about their pre-existing medical history, their injuries and the impact of the same on their daily activities and work, home and social life. Instructions must be corroborated by the medical records and where they are not, clear instructions will need to be taken.

Defendant practitioners should carefully consider the expert specialisms that have been instructed by the Claimant and ensure they are necessary and required for resolution of the proceedings. Practitioners should also consider the medical records and whether any additional specialisms ought to be instructed.

Liability

The experts instructed to deal with liability will depend on the circumstances leading up to the amputation and the specialisms involved in the Claimant's care. It is not uncommon for experts in orthopaedics and vascular surgery to be instructed in amputation cases. It is also important to consider the impact of any underlying health conditions on the Claimant's injuries and whether any additional specialisms are required to give evidence. For example, in the case of a Claimant with a history of diabetes it is likely that evidence will be needed from an endocrinologist on the risk of amputation occurring in any event because it is recognised that people with diabetes are at a much higher risk of needing an amputation than those that do not.

Where an amputation was carried out as an emergency procedure, the risk of serious complications is higher than where a planned amputation is carried out. Complications can include infection, deep vein thrombosis, pain, neuroma and phantom phenomenon. In cases where amputation has taken place recently, it is important for practitioners to pay attention to the Claimant's condition in the post-operative period and for experts to consider the likelihood of any complications occurring. Future deterioration and life-expectancy will also need to be considered by the experts. It is also important to look at the future risk of amputations not only in respect of the amputated limb, but also the non-amputated limb.

Quantum

Undergoing an amputation is a life-changing event and adjusting to life afterwards can be extremely difficult for the Claimant. It is important for Claimants to have access to the necessary treatment and support required for their recovery. The principle of compensation is to put a Claimant back into the position they would have been in, but for the negligence and as such, Claimant practitioners should bear in mind the Claimant's lifestyle prior to the alleged negligence and whether they had any active hobbies or sports and ensure this is dealt with by the appropriate expert.

A Claimant will require input from different specialisms to assist with their recovery and rehabilitation including but not limited to:-

- Psychology/psychiatry
- Rehabilitation
- Prosthetics
- Care and case management
- Occupational therapy
- Physiotherapy
- Accommodation
- Assistive technology

Losing a limb can be devastating and will have a significant psychological impact on a Claimant. It is likely that an expert will need to be instructed to comment on whether a psychiatric injury has been caused by the alleged negligence. The expert should consider the impact of any pre-existing psychological conditions and the Claimant's future trajectory and whether treatment is required. It is important to consider the circumstances leading up to the amputation, for example was the amputation planned or an emergency? In the case of the latter, a Claimant may not have had much or any time to mentally prepare for the loss of a limb which may have severe psychological consequences for them.

A Claimant's physical rehabilitation is vital to their recovery, therefore it is imperative for a rehabilitation expert to assess them and devise a programme for their rehabilitation.

The care expert will comment on the Claimant's care needs. Input from an occupational therapist will be needed to confirm future aids and equipment that will be needed and the costs of the same. They will also be able to advise on whether property adaptations are required. It is likely that a Claimant's house will need to be adapted to their needs. It is important for the accommodation expert to comment on the suitability of the current property and adaptations that will be required, or whether a new property ought to be purchased. They will need to understand the Claimant's needs and therefore, will need to be provided with all evidence on the Claimant's condition and prognosis, their care needs, therapies and aids and equipment. A report from an assistive technology expert may be required.

A prosthetics expert will be required to assess the Claimant's prosthetic needs. Having a prosthetic limb can be physically demanding because the amputee has to compensate for the loss of muscle and bone in their amputated limb. Prosthetics will not be suitable for every Claimant, therefore it is important for a Defendant practitioner to consider the Claimant's health and their suitability for a prosthetic limb. That said, even if an injured person cannot physically cope with a functional prosthetic limb, they may still wish to have a cosmetic limb.

Prosthetics are expensive and the type of prosthetic is often contested. If the Claimant is already using a certain prosthetic and can evidence the benefit from that, it will be difficult for a judge to award a different type of prosthetic. Therefore, where liability has been admitted, it is recommended for interim damages payments to be secured as early as possible so that prosthetics can be purchased and trialled.

Where a Claimant is undergoing therapies, it is important to consider the treating therapists' recommendations and whether these are also supported by the experts.

Experts are vital to the success of a case therefore it is important to ensure the correct experts are instructed and tested thoroughly throughout the life of the case.

References

1. Stewart, C.P.U. (2008) *Synopsis of Causation: Lower Limb Amputation*. Ministry of Defence. Available at: https://assets.publishing.service.gov.uk/media/5a756e8ded915d74e33f1d8e/lower-limb-amputation.pdf (assets.publishing.service.gov.uk in Bing)

CHAPTER THREE

EXPERT EVIDENCE: AVOIDING PITFALLS

Expert evidence is essential to evaluate and explain medical issues in amputation claims. It is important to balance obtaining permission to rely on experts from all relevant areas against proportionality and the overriding objective.

Expert evidence will make or break a case and there are a number of things that practitioners can do to avoid falling into their opponent's traps.

First, practitioners should ensure that their expert is suitably qualified to be giving the evidence. When approaching experts, practitioners should ask for a CV so that they can be satisfied the experts have the qualifications and expertise to comment on the necessary issues. It is important to check the expert's experience and whether this is current. This is especially important with experts that are reporting on breach of duty. Practitioners should ensure the experts were practising at the time of the alleged negligence and check their opponent's expert's qualifications. Practitioners may also want to check with colleagues of their experience with various experts.

It is important that the expert clearly sets out their relevant qualifications and experience in their report. This can help with avoiding or limiting any challenges to their qualifications.

In the case of *Sycurio Ltd v PCI-PAL plc EWCA Civ 606*, the Judge made it clear that experts must be a genuine expert in the relevant field. The Judge said:

> *"'An expert is not instructed for court proceedings on the basis that they believe that they have "sufficient" grasp of the matter to express a view, or are able to teach themselves what they need to know in the course of preparing their evidence. They are instructed on the basis that they are a genuine expert in the relevant field, whose opinions may be relied upon and given weight by the Court."*

It is important to consider whether the expert is published in the area they are being asked to comment on. If they are, this will go towards their credibility and to their authority on the subject area.

It's important to ensure that expert evidence is tested at key stages throughout the case. Test the evidence before you put your statement of case to your opponent, when you receive your opponent's statement of case and as and when you receive evidence from them. Practitioners should consider any potential weaknesses in the case with the experts as early as possible.

Experts must be reminded their duty is to the Court. They must provide an independent opinion. They must be aware of and understand their duties and refer to the relevant expert guidance as set out in CPR 35. Reports must be CPR compliant. Any literature referred to should be provided with reports.

Parties should ensure reports are thorough, supported by relevant literature or data and that experts are willing to stand by their conclusions under cross-examination. Causation can be a challenging with amputations claims and the expert evidence will be key to the Court's determination of causation of a Claimant's amputation as demonstrated by the case of *Appleton v Medway NHS Foundation Trust [2013] EWHC 4776 (QB), [2013] All ER (D) 93 (Nov).*

In the case of *Appleton v Medway*, the Claimant's expert relied on literature to support his position. The Court noted that textbooks and articles could be used to support a party's position, but it was not there to substitute direct evidence. The context of literature may not always be clear and the Court must decide cases based on the evidence which is heard. In the case of *Breeze v Ahmad [2005] EWCA Civ 223*, the Court found that the Trial judge had placed more weight on the literature referred to by the Defendant's expert than was appropriate.

Experts should be encouraged to undertake a literature search as early as possible in a case. They should consider all relevant literature and they should not selectively present it to support their argument. Thorough research reviews should be undertaken as early as possible. This can avoid a situation where your opponent finds literature closer to trial which will then need to be considered with your expert. This may result in procedural or costs difficulties where your expert reviews their position closer to trial and locates new literature which your opponent has not seen.

Where expert evidence is relied on for quantum, the points above still apply. For example, practitioners should ensure that therapists or care experts have experience of implementing therapies or care regimes for amputees. Expert opinions should be sought on the recommendations of treating therapists and in the case of prosthetics, these should be trialled with the experts.

Factual evidence

The factual evidence should address any relevant pre-existing condition.

Where future treatment is recommended, the factual evidence should address this and the intention to undergo treatment. Importantly, where prosthetics are recommended the factual evidence should address the Claimant's intention to use a prosthetic. If an interim payment has been secured, the Claimant should seek to trial a prosthetic and record the trial so that it can be submitted as evidence of use.

The factual evidence must be provided to the experts. This is to ensure they are aware of the Claimant's individual circumstances which must be taken into account by the expert and their evidence should be tailored to the specific facts and context of the case, including the Claimant's unique situation and medical history. This approach ensures that the evidence is relevant and accurately reflects the Claimant's condition and needs.

Once factual evidence is exchanged, your opponent's evidence should be reviewed by your expert.

The process of exchanging factual witness evidence can lead to further challenges in the case. Experts may need to reconsider their preliminary opinions based on new factual evidence, which can result in differing accounts of events. This can make it difficult for the Court to ascertain the truth, as experts are limited to indicating the probability of events based on scientific or medical reasoning, rather than making factual determinations.

The pitfalls of factual evidence in amputation claims can revolve around the challenges in establishing causation and the reliability of witness testimony. The case of *Appleton v Medway NHS Foundation Trust* highlights the difficulty in proving causation when expert opinions diverge and factual evidence is inconclusive.

Similarly, in *Tuffin v University Hospitals Coventry & Warwickshire NHS Trust [2024] EWHC 3318 (KB)*, the Court faced challenges in determining the cause of the amputation. The evidence included detailed contemporaneous documentation and expert testimony, yet there was no consensus on whether the Claimant's amputation resulted from the Defendant's negligence. This case demonstrates the complexity of relying on factual evidence, as even comprehensive medical records and expert opinions may not definitively establish causation.

In summary, the pitfalls of factual evidence in amputation claims include the challenges in proving causation due to conflicting expert opinions and the difficulties in relying on witness testimony and medical records to establish a clear sequence of events leading to the amputation.

Proving causation can be challenging. The judgment in *Aaron Haley v Newcold Ltd [2025] EWCC 57* references principles of causation and this case considered whether a novus actus interveniens – a new intervening act, broke the chain of causation.

The court considered whether the Claimant's below knee amputation in 2024 was caused by an accident at work which occurred in 2019.

The Claimant was involved in an accident at work where he suffered a severe crush injury to his right foot after being struck by a forklift truck. The Claimant underwent multiple surgeries and eventually underwent an elective amputation in March 2024. The Claimant claimed the amputation was necessary due to "unbearable" pain and loss of function. He argued that the elective amputation was justified on the basis that he was suffering from chronic pain and functional limitations.

The court was asked to determine a preliminary issue as to whether the elective below knee amputation in March 2024 was caused by the accident in March 2019. Surveillance evidence was produced by the Defendant showing the Claimant carrying out various activities and the Defendant highlighted that the medical records reflected a relatively good level of function.

The Defendant submitted that the decision to undergo the amputation was personal rather than medically required, as such there was no causative link between the accident and the amputation. The psychiatric experts agreed that the Claimant was not suffering from a mental health condition such as severe depression or PTSD which would make the amputation a therapeutic necessity. The court found no compelling psychiatric evidence to support the Claimant's decision. The judgment noted:

> *"I am satisfied that the Claimant had improved and was effectively functioning normally in the months and weeks prior to amputation, his conduct in seeking amputation is so wholly unreasonable and/or of such overwhelming impact, that it eclipses the Defendant's wrongdoing and breaks the chain of causation".*

The courts approach reinforces that elective amputations must be supported by clear clinical and psychological justifications to support the causal link to the original injury. Psychological evidence must be considered carefully when determining whether the Claimant's choice is reasonable or amounts to a novus actus interveniens. When considering a claim where elective surgery is as a consequence of accident-related trauma, robust psychiatric assessment should be undertaken and considered carefully.

This finding is significant because psychological distress often plays an important role in elective amputation cases. Claimants who experience chronic pain combined with psychological deterioration may argue that surgery was necessary to cope with the injuries. However, in the case of *Hayley v Newcold Limited*, the medical and surveillance evidence ultimately undermined the Claimant of debilitating pain and psychological suffering.

Fundamental Dishonesty

In amputation claims, the fundamentally dishonest Claimant could be exaggerating the severity of their injuries, fabricating the need for certain prosthetics or misrepresenting the impact of the amputation on their daily life. It is important that a Claimant's evidence is thoroughly tested and expert assessments must be thorough to substantiate the extent of the injury and its impact.

It is for a Defendant to prove fundamental dishonesty and they must provide clear evidence if allegations of fundamental dishonesty are being made. If surveillance is undertaken, it must be obtained and disclosed in a timely and proportionate matter. Surveillance evidence can be crucial to proving fundamental dishonesty and it is persuasive where a significant and deliberate exaggeration of symptoms is demonstrated. The degree of exaggeration and the context in which it occurs is important; gross exaggeration or dishonesty undermines the integrity of the claim. Courts have the authority to dismiss an entire claim under section 57 of the Criminal Justice and Courts Act 2015 if fundamental dishonesty is established, even if only part of the claim is dishonest.

In addition to surveillance footage, social media accounts may also be accessed to demonstrate fundamental dishonesty.

Claimants should be warned of the consequences if they are found to be fundamentally dishonest which can include dismissal of their claim, an order to pay the costs of both sides, criminal prosecution, loss of the protection of Qualified One-way Cost Shifting and sentencing for contempt of Court. Claimants must be honest and accurate and transparent; if their condition is up and down then this must be explained in the evidence clearly.

References

1. Goldsmith Chambers (2019) *What NOT to do as an Expert Witness: From a Barrister's Point of View*. Goldsmith Chambers. Available at: https://www.goldsmithchambers.com/wp-content/uploads/2019/11/What-NOT-to-do-as-an-Expert-Witness-from-a-Barristers-point-of-view.pdf (goldsmithchambers.com in Bing)

2. LexisNexis (n.d.) *Analytical material – UK* [online]. Lexis+. Available at: https://plus.lexis.com/document?pddocfullpath=%2fshared%2fdocument%2fanalytical-materials-uk%2furn%3acontentItem%3a8TB1-9HF2-D6MY-P21C-00000-00&pdmfid=1001073&pdcontentcomponentid=434922&pdproductcontenttypeid=urn:pct:237&pdisdoclinkaccess=true&pdischatbotdoc=true&passagetext=

CHAPTER FOUR

PSYCHOLOGICAL IMPACT

The psychological effects of an amputation can significantly affect an individual's quality of life. Amputation is not merely a physical loss, the psychological consequences can also significantly affect functionality and identity.

It is essential for practitioners to understand the mental health implications and rehabilitation needs and ensure these are accurately assessed in order for the injured party to obtain fair compensation.

A range of emotional responses can be triggered as a result of an amputation. These can include but are not limited to, anxiety, depression and grief. Research suggests that approximately 35% of amputees experience clinical depression following a leg amputation.

Patients who have undergone trauma related amputations such as road traffic accidents and workplace injuries may be more greatly affected, psychologically, than those who have undergone elected surgical procedures.

Some mental health difficulties faced by Claimants include social isolation, which can occur as a result of reduced mobility and perceived social stigma.

The role of the psychological medico-legal expert should be to provide a diagnosis and consider factors such as depression and PTSD. When providing a prognosis, treatment needs should also be considered as should the impact of the Claimant's capacity.

Capacity

Capacity should always be at the forefront of any practitioner's mind when dealing with litigation. Particularly if acting for the Claimant. The Mental Capacity Act 2005 states that a person must be assumed to have capacity unless it is established that he lacks capacity. The person is not to be treated as unable to make decisions unless all practicable steps to help him to do so have been undertaken without success. A person is not to be treated as unable to make a decision merely because he makes an unwise decision.

Therefore, as soon as instructions are accepted - and throughout the life of the claim, consideration should be given to remaining alert if there are any doubts about capacity. Practitioners should consider the Claimant's ability to make decisions and retain information. They should also consider the Claimant's ability to weigh up information and communicate their decisions. If there are any doubts, the Claimant should be referred for a formal assessment.

The cases below highlight some issues that may arise relating to capacity in amputation claims.

The case of *King's College Hospital NHS Foundation Trust v South London and Maudsley NHS Foundation Trust & Anor [2024] EWCOP 20* considered whether it was in the Claimant's best interests to have his ulcerated leg amputated.

This case involved a 60-year-old gentleman who at the time had a history of paranoid schizophrenia. He was taken to hospital by his niece and was suffering with severe infection and necrotic ulcers on his right leg. It was considered that failure to treat these would have been fatal.

The case considered whether the Claimant lacked capacity to make decisions about his medical treatment including whether or not he had capacity to consent to the amputation and whether the surgery was in the Claimant's best interests under the Mental Capacity Act 2005. The medical evidence presented, recommended the above knee amputation.

Having considered all the medical evidence, the court found that the Claimant lacked capacity under the Mental Capacity Act 2005. It was considered that the above knee amputation was in the Claimant's best interests. However, it was emphasised that a person is not deemed unable to make a decision simply on the basis of making an unwise decision. This decision took into consideration the Claimant's expressed wishes and balanced these against the need to save his life. The Claimant had previously expressed a desire to live. The judge applied the best interest test and concluded the only feasible option to save the Claimant's life was to proceed with the amputation.

In the case of *Pennine Acute Hospitals NHS Trust v TM [2021] EWCOP 8* a homeless man presented with severe frost bite leading to necrosis in both legs. A bilateral below knee amputation was advised by medical professionals as lifesaving treatment. The Claimant did not want to undergo the amputation. The Claimant's mental capacity was assessed and it was found that whilst he understood the nature of the procedure, he was unable to rationally weigh up the risks and benefits as a result of his impaired reasoning which was influenced by his mental state. The court found in favour of the surgery because it was in the Claimant's best interests to prevent imminent death. The judge noted:

> *"In some cases, there would be information from family members that might cast light on his thinking and beliefs. Here none is available. However, TM's instinctive enthusiasm for the natural word, his pride in and love for his daughter and his spontaneous expression of his wish to see her, indicate to me a man who would choose to live."*

The judge stressed that it is vital to distinguish between simply understanding information and being able to use and weigh that information when making a decision. He also confirmed that if a patient lacks capacity, their refusal of life-saving treatment can be lawfully overridden

In contrast, in the case of *ZA. An NHS Foundation Trust v ZA (by her litigation friend the Official Solicitor), [2021] EWCOP.*

The Claimant had suffered from a long history of acute schizophrenia and had also been diagnosed with Type II diabetes. Her diabetes complications led her to develop foot ulcers and osteomyelitis. Her treating clinicians advised the Claimant to have an above knee amputation and considered that without this, her life expectancy would be limited. The issue regarding the Claimant's capacity was not contested. Evidence suggested that she had consistently refused the amputation since 2016, a time when she retained capacity. The court considered the Claimant's long-standing wishes against surgery and noted while there was a strong presumption in favour of preserving life it was not absolute (*Aintree University Hospital NHS Foundation Trust v Jones (2013) UK SC67*). The court took into consideration the effect the amputation would have on the claimant's quality of life and considering all the information concluded that the above knee amputation was not in the Claimant's best interest.

It is important to note that each case will be considered on its own merit and the Claimants' preferences will be taken into consideration carefully. This will ultimately be balanced against the overall welfare and medical opinions but at the heart of the decision making is the Claimant's best interests and ensuring that their wishes are taken into consideration.

The above cases emphasise the fact that capacity must be assessed specifically for the decision in question and best interests include medical necessity and the individuals' expressed wishes.

References

1. Donovan-Hall, M.K., Yardley, L. and Watts, R.J., 2002. Engagement in activities revealing the body and psychosocial adjustment in adults with a trans-tibial prosthesis. Prosthetics and Orthotics International, 26, pp.15–22

2. Jo, S.H., Kang, S.H., Seo, W.S., Koo, B.H., Kim, H.G. and Yun, S.H., 2021. Psychiatric understanding and treatment of patients with amputations. Yeungnam University Journal of Medicine, 38(3), pp.194–201.

CHAPTER FIVE

HEADS OF LOSS

Once a Claimant has been assessed by the relevant medical experts, practitioners should be in a position to quantify the claim.

The purpose of compensation in personal injury and clinical negligence claims is to put the Claimant back in the position they would have been but for the negligence. Therefore, it is important that a thorough assessment of the Claimant's injuries is undertaken and supported by medical experts' opinion.

Damages are quantified in two parts: general damages and special damages

General damages take into account the Claimant's pain, suffering and loss of amenity (PSLA) resulting from the amputation. Factors to consider when assessing an appropriate award include physical pain, psychological injury, the impact on a Claimant's life and hobbies and quality of life. The starting point when quantifying damages is the Judicial College Guidelines (JCG). The purpose of the JCG is to ensure a consistent approach is taken when valuing claims. The guidelines consider a wide range of injuries and valuations.

The guidelines are updated over time to consider extenuating factors such as inflation. This is to ensure that the figures quoted within the guidelines remain as up to date as possible.

The JCG and relevant case law should be a practitioner's starting point when considering the value of a claim for pain, suffering and loss of amenity.

Special damages are quantifiable financial losses that have been incurred as a result of the negligence.

Past special damages awards in amputation cases can include loss of earnings, travel expenses, care and assistance, case management, home adaptations, aids and equipment, prosthetics and other financial losses incurred. These claims must be supported with documentary evidence such as receipts and invoices where possible.

The most significant part of the award usually involves the future losses, which includes loss of earnings, pension loss, long-term care needs, case management, accommodation (including adaptations) and increased utilities, prosthetics (including insurance costs and replacement of prosthesis) and equipment (including their replacement).

The Schedule of Loss should contain as much detail as reasonably practical and should identify those losses that are ongoing. When serving the Schedule of Loss at the preliminary stage, practitioners may not have obtained all expert evidence to be able to fully quantify the claim. Therefore, if the Schedule of Loss is likely to be updated before the case is concluded as in the majority of cases, it should clearly state this.

It may be many months, if not years, particularly in medical negligence claims, before a Schedule of Loss can be finalised. Therefore, if acting for the Claimant it is important to highlight the need to keep any receipts or evidence in support of any losses that have been incurred from an early stage. If members of the Claimant's family are also providing extensive care, it may be sensible to keep a diary which can assist with preparing the quantum witness statements or care expert instructions.

The purpose of the Schedule of Loss is to provide a detailed breakdown of any past and future losses with evidence in support. Each head of loss should be carefully set out within the Schedule of Loss with a clear explanation of what is being claimed and why. If there is expert evidence in support of the head of loss, then reference to that evidence should also be included.

The more detailed the Schedule of Loss, the more prepared practitioners will be for any offers that may arise throughout the case. A detailed Schedule of Loss will also allow the Defendant the opportunity to understand the level of claim that is being brought.

The cases which often achieve the best outcome are those which are drafted in a realistic manner and supported by evidence. An inflated Schedule of Loss undermines the case and will lose credibility. Further, the Claimant will have to sign a Statement of Truth to verify that the content is accurate. If that content has been exaggerated then this can lead to allegations of fundamental dishonesty which can have serious implications for the Claimant as discussed earlier.

CHAPTER SIX

INTERIM PAYMENTS

Some personal injury or medical negligence cases may take a number of years to conclude, therefore in all cases where liability has been admitted, an interim payment should be sought as soon as possible to facilitate any immediate needs the Claimant may have. These needs can include but are not limited to prosthetics and rehabilitation, care and accommodation.

Where liability is admitted an interim payment may be made without the need for an application, if agreed between the Parties. However, in cases involving protected parties, the Claimant will need Court approval even if the amount has been agreed.

Civil Procedure Rule 25.7(1) notes that:

> *Applications must be supported in the following form unless the court, a rule, a practice direction or an enactment requires an affidavit -*
>
> *a) A witness statement*
>
> *b) A Statement of Case; or*
>
> *c) The application.*

(2) The evidence must set out all the relevant facts.

CPR 25.22 (1) notes that an application for an interim payment order must be supported by evidence dealing with the sum of money sought by way of an interim payment and in claims for personal injuries, details of special damages and past and future loss.

As such, the court will require a careful breakdown of the amount sought and evidence in support of the same.

CPR 25.23 states that the Court may only make an interim payment order where any of the following conditions are satisfied—

> *(a) the defendant against whom the order is sought has admitted liability to pay damages or another sum of money to the claimant;*
>
> *(b) the claimant has obtained judgment against that defendant for damages to be assessed, or for another sum of money (other than costs) to be assessed;*
>
> *(c) it is satisfied that, if the claim went to trial, the claimant would obtain judgment for a substantial amount of money (other than costs) against the defendant from whom they are seeking an interim payment, whether or not that defendant is the only defendant or one of several;*
>
> *(e) the claimant is seeking an order for possession of land (whether or not any other order is also sought), and the court is satisfied that, if the case went to trial, the defendant would be held liable (even if the claim for possession fails) to pay the claimant a sum of money for the defendant's occupation and use of the land while the claim for possession was pending; or*
>
> *(f) there are two or more defendants and the order is sought against any one or more of them, and—*

> (i) *the court is satisfied that, if the claim went to trial, the claimant would obtain judgment for a substantial amount of money (other than costs) against at least one of the defendants (but the court cannot determine which); and*
>
> (ii) *all the defendants are either public bodies; or insured in respect of the claim or are defendants whose liability will be met by an insurer under section 151 of the Road Traffic Act 1988(5), or an insurer acting under the Motor Insurers Bureau Agreement, or the Motor Insurers Bureau where it is acting itself.*

The Court of Appeal provided relevant guidance in *Eeles v Cobham Hire Services Limited [2009] EWCA Civ 204*. The Court looked at a two-stage test:

Stage 1 assesses the likely amount of final damages, excluding future losses likely to be the subject of Periodical Payment Orders.

> *"The judge's first task is to assess the likely amount of the final judgment, leaving out of account the heads of future loss which the trial judge might wish to deal with by PPO. Strictly speaking, the assessment should comprise only special damages to date and damages for pain, suffering and loss of amenity, with interest on both. However, we consider that the practice of awarding accommodation costs (including future running costs) as a lump sum is sufficiently well established that it will usually be appropriate to include accommodation costs in the expected capital award. The assessment should be carried out on a conservative basis. Save in the circumstances discussed below, the interim payment will be a reasonable proportion of that assessment. A reasonable proportion may well be a high proportion, provided that the assessment has been*

> *conservative. The objective is not to keep the claimant out of his money but to avoid any risk of over-payment."*

Stage 2: The Court must be satisfied to a high degree of confidence that there is a real need for the amount identified now as opposed to after trial and the amount requested is reasonable.

> *"We turn to the circumstances in which the judge will be entitled to include in his assessment of the likely amount of the final judgment additional elements of future loss. That can be done when the judge can confidently predict that the trial judge will wish to award a larger capital sum than that covered by general and special damages, interest and accommodation costs alone. We endorse the approach of Stanley Burnton J in Braithwaite. Before taking such a course, the judge must be satisfied by evidence that there is a real need for the interim payment requested. For example, where the request is for money to buy a house, he must be satisfied that there is a real need for accommodation now (as opposed to after the trial) and that the amount of money requested is reasonable. He does not need to decide whether the particular house proposed is suitable; that is a matter for the Court of Protection. But the judge must not make an interim payment order without first deciding whether expenditure of approximately the amount he proposes to award is reasonably necessary. If the judge is satisfied of that, to a high degree of confidence, then he will be justified in predicting that the trial judge would take that course and he will be justified in assessing the likely amount of the final award at such a level as will permit the making of the necessary interim award."*

In the case of PAL (a child) -v- Davison and Ors [2021] EWHC 1108 (QB), the Court considered the Claimant's interim application on behalf of a child who had suffered catastrophic injury. Liability was not an issue.

The Claimant had obtained some medical evidence including a report from a paediatric neurologist which confirmed a final prognosis could not be given until the Claimant reached seventeen years of age.

The Claimant's accommodation expert, Mr Wethers had also prepared a report:

> *"In an addendum report dated March 2021, he noted that the family had struggled to find suitable accommodation and indicated that his research identified a lack of appropriate accommodation in the area where the claimant currently lives. He advised that the identified property could be altered and extended to meet the claimant's needs."*

The Defendants had not sought any expert evidence before the Claimant's application was made:

> *"In his skeleton argument, Mr O'Sullivan QC observed that the hearing of this application had been expedited and the defendants had had less than three weeks to respond to the evidence served by the claimant."*

In this case the Claimant had already received interim payments totaling £1,025,000. The Claimant sought a further interim payment of £2 million in order for suitable accommodation to be purchased and adapted. The test in Eeles was applied

The judge concluded

> *"It follows that once I have decided that it is necessary to purchase a property for the claimant now, the only available option is the property which has been identified and for which*

> *a purchase price of £1,190,000 has been agreed. That price is within the range originally identified as appropriate by Mr Wethers, albeit at the upper end of the range. I am not deciding that the claimant should purchase that property nor am I deciding that the claimant will ultimately be entitled to damages assessed on the basis of that property. I do though consider that looking at the viable options today, it is reasonably necessary to incur the expenditure proposed in order to secure what appears to be the only available property to meet the claimant's needs....*
>
> *It follows from the above that I am satisfied, applying the second stage of Eeles, that I should order an interim payment in the sum of £2million and I do so"*

The Defendant in PAL had three weeks to respond to the application and did not have expert accommodation evidence to be able to do this, however the Judge was unsympathetic to this.

A common theme running through the case law is the importance of supportive expert evidence. It is essential for the Claimant to line up quantum expert evidence at the earliest possible opportunity if liability is admitted. This evidence will assist with negotiating interim payments. Such evidence is also likely to satisfy a judge at an application hearing that the proposed interim payment is necessary.

If it is likely that the Claimant may suggest their pre-injury accommodation is unsuitable and/or there are indications that more suitable accommodation is being explored, the Defendant should seek to obtain their own expert evidence at that point.

Where possible, Claimant practitioners should consider the potential for interim payments at the outset. As with the majority of catastrophic injury cases there is a significant financial burden placed on the Claimant and therefore it is essential to identify the Claimant's needs as early as possible, ideally before those needs become urgent or critical.

Engaging in open conversations with your opponent are also worth exploring.

There is no limit on the amount of interim payment applications a Claimant can make. Therefore, if a case is difficult to quantify and the total amount of compensation recoverable is uncertain, it may be worth considering whether it is appropriate to make a number of smaller applications until the position regarding quantum calculations become clearer.

CHAPTER SEVEN

REHABILITATION

The purpose of personal injury or medical negligence litigation is to restore the individual, in so far as possible, to their position before the injury.

Major limb amputation impacts hugely on an individual. It is a life changing event. Early rehabilitation can result in a faster recovery period and can also benefit the individual in the long term, potentially avoiding further complications or worsening of symptoms that may present in the future.

The parties should not lose sight of the individual at the heart of this process. When a Claimant sustains a life changing injury such as an amputation, their world is turned upside down. It's not uncommon for amputees' self-esteem to be impacted as they struggle to come to terms with the physical and psychological impacts of limb loss. Their day-to-day life has been impacted, as well as their relationships with others.

The financial strain of a catastrophic injury has a huge impact not only on the individual but also on family members. Many individuals cannot work, or at least are no longer able to work in the roles they were in prior to their injuries. In addition, family members may have to stop working to care for the injured party.

Depending on the nature of the injury, early rehabilitation may enable a Claimant to return to work sooner. This not only benefits the individual but also offers advantages to the Defendant, who may have to meet a reduced loss of earnings claim as a result.

What is the Rehabilitation Code?

The Rehabilitation Code 2015 ("the Code") encourages practitioners to work collaboratively to put rehabilitation in place, as early as possible, to ensure an injured person makes the best recovery.

The purpose of the Code is to provide a framework for personal injury and clinical negligence claims.

Both parties are encouraged to use the Code, and it is important to note that it can be applied even if there is no admission on liability. Engaging with the Code is voluntary, however both the Pre-Action Protocol for Personal Injury Claims and Pre- Action Protocol for Resolution of Clinical Disputes encourage the parties to consider the Claimant's rehabilitation needs as soon as possible. Therefore, Defendant practitioners should consider prospects from an early stage, particularly in personal injury cases. If there is likely to be a partial admission pending evidence, it would seem sensible to engage in the rehabilitation process given the health and economic benefits.

Claimant solicitor's obligations

The Code requires the Claimant solicitor to consult closely with the Claimant and their family and treating clinicians (where reasonable and proportionate to do so) in carrying out their duties. The Claimant solicitor's obligations are set out in Part 2 of the 2015 Code. The following points below are an expansion on the 2007 Code. These include:

- Acting in the best interests of their client beyond just securing reasonable financial compensation;

- Considering whether early intervention, rehabilitation or medical treatment may improve the claimant's present and/ or future needs

- Addressing whether the Claimant can continue their employment and communicating this with the Defendant

- Providing the Defendant with sufficient information to enable them to assess the need for rehabilitation assistance and likely continuing disability.

- Working collaboratively with the Defendant discussing suggestion for rehabilitation, early intervention or medical treatment and responding to the Defendant within 21 days

- Considering the appointment of a case manager where appropriate.

The code encourages Defendants to:

- Consider, as early as possible, whether any medical or rehabilitative treatment would be beneficial to the Claimant.

- If it is considered that the Claimant may have rehabilitation needs, the Claimant's representative should be contacted promptly and a collaborative approach is encouraged to address those needs.

- If the Claimant has rehabilitation needs, any request for rehabilitation should be responded to within 21 days, either confirming the request or rejecting it. If the request is rejected, reasons should be set out as to why.

Assessment process – for medium, severe and catastrophic injuries.

- Both parties should consider the choice of the assessor to carry out an Immediate Needs Assessment (INA). The parties have 21 days in which to object to any nominated assessor and are also expected to agree the method (for example joint or single instruction) of providing instructions to the assessor to carry out an immediate needs assessment report ("the report").

- The report should not comment on any issues relating to liability. Having said that, it should allow the parties to understand the circumstances which the injury occurred. For the rehabilitation process to work in the spirit that it was intended, the report should be of benefit to both parties. It should be sent to both parties simultaneously, following which either party will have an opportunity to ask the assessor questions about the report.

- Unless both parties agree in writing, the report should be used wholly outside the litigation process. However, any notes or reports prepared during the case management process will be covered by the parties' duty of disclosure.

Assessor's Recommendations

After having received the INA report the Defendant should respond to the Claimant Solicitor within 21 days setting out a response to include the following:

1. Whether the recommendations within the report can be accepted and if so to what extent they are willing to fund treatment.

2. Rejecting the recommendations but setting out justifications for the same.

3. The Defendant is not required to pay for any treatment or rehabilitation which is considered to be unreasonable. The Claimant is also required to consider the treatment options but is not expected to undergo any treatment which is considered to be unreasonable.

4. If a Claimant decides to take up a more expensive treatment option, this should be supported by evidence if the Claimant is hoping to recover the additional cost. The reasonableness of the Claimant's decision will be taken into account on the assessment of damages.

5. Should the claim fail or contributory negligence be alleged, the Defendant should not seek to recoup the cost of treatment funding which has already been agreed and put in place. However, this is subject to any allegation of fraud / fundamental dishonesty.

The benefit of an early Immediate Needs Assessment enables the Defendant to assess the likely value of the claim at an early stage and consider real issues that the Claimant is facing. This information does not usually become available until medical expert evidence is served which can be many months, if not years later. However, in cases where liability is denied, this is more challenging; the Defendant may not wish to engage in the rehabilitation code. This can be true in clinical negligence cases where it may take many months, if not years before liability can be resolved. The Code has clearly taken such cases into account. It recognises that the health and economic benefits of proceedings with rehabilitation at an early stage, regardless of agreement on liability, may be especially strong in catastrophic and in other severe cases.

Timely rehabilitation can benefit the Claimant with a saving in damages to the Defendant resulting from the better recovery the Claimant has made. In addition, working collaboratively can also achieve an earlier settlement.

Claimant solicitors should be encouraged to communicate with the Defendant at an early stage. If a full Letter of Claim cannot be drafted, then a Letter of Notification setting out the initial aspects of the claim together with the severity of the injury should be provided. In cases where liability is admitted an interim payment can be requested at an early stage, thereby alleviating some of the financial difficulty.

In cases where liability is not straightforward or denied, the Defendant may be less willing to engage in the rehabilitation process. A Defendant may refuse to instruct a case manager for an Immediate Needs Assessment or if willing to agree a jointly instructed case manager, may then not be willing to fund early rehabilitation on the basis that liability is in dispute. In cases where liability is denied and there are sufficient prospects to issue Court proceedings, this may be the best way to proceed. This will allow issues between the parties to be identified sooner, thereby avoiding delay in progressing the claim and a Claimant's access to funds.

In medical negligence cases liability is not straight forward and the parties will have to review all the medical records and obtain their own expert evidence before a decision on liability is made. However, even in cases where a breach of duty is admitted, causation may remain disputed. This approach inevitably delays any rehabilitation.

Early rehabilitation can help reduce the impact and pressure on the NHS. Where there has been no engagement with the Code or no interim payments are forthcoming, Claimants will have to rely on NHS treatment. However, the NHS is under significant strain and access to treatment can often be a postcode lottery. Delayed access to rehabilitation has an impact on the Claimant's physical and mental health and can often cause further distress during an already challenging time.

While no amount of compensation can restore the Claimant to their pre-accident condition—particularly in cases involving catastrophic injury—early rehabilitation can make a profound difference in improving their quality of life. It is therefore essential that both parties remain mindful of the Rehabilitation Code from the outset, and engage in early, constructive discussions around rehabilitation. Prompt intervention not only supports recovery but also reflects a collaborative and responsible approach to litigation.

References

1. Source Lexis PSL Personal injury Practical Guidance Rehabilitation Code 2015

CHAPTER EIGHT

ADVANCEMENTS IN PROSTHESIS TECHNOLOGY AND RECOVERABILITY

Prosthetics have come a long way from the papier-mache 'Greville Chester Toe' and the 'Cairo Toe' made from wood and leather. Scientists have been developing robotics, artificial intelligence, virtual reality, and motion-sensing technologies for prosthetics. Such developments allow amputees to lead much more independent lives.

Below we discuss some of the technological advancements made in this area.

Bionic or Microprocessor-controlled prosthetics

Microprocessor-controlled or bionic prosthetics use advanced sensors and microprocessors to analyse the electrical signals produced by the user's muscles. They can be used to perform tasks such as gripping objects, typing on a keyboard and can also be used when playing sports. Bionic limbs enhance movement and dexterity, which can help amputees regain functionality and improve their overall quality of life.

Microprocessor controlled knees use a battery- powered, built-in, programmable computer that continuously controls both swing and stance phase based on real time data of the user's gait.

Claims for microprocessor/bionic limb technology will be contentious, although it is recognised that a microprocessor knee is appropriate for above knee amputees because it offers stability and therefore is safer than a traditional prosthetic. Having an expert recommendation for these types of prosthetics is a starting point but there must be a reasonable requirement for them, and the costs claimed also have to be reasonable.

Osseointegration

Osseointegration is a surgical technique that involves the integration of a prosthetic limb directly into the bone using a metal implant, allowing for improved stability, increased load-bearing capacity, and enhanced sensory feedback. This technology aims to overcome the challenges associated with socket prosthetics, offering greater comfort, improved mobility, and a more natural walking gait.

Residual limb shrinkage can occur over a couple of years post-amputation and can impact the fit of the socket and can lead to the need for frequent refitting of sockets. This can be expensive. Sockets can result in sweating, skin irritation, sores, ulcers and infection which may lead to revision surgery being required. There can also be pain and discomfort which may impact how long a prosthetic is worn. Osseointegration can be more beneficial than the more traditional socket prosthesis. They can offer greater comfort, a more natural walking gait and improved mobility. That said, there are risks of infection and bone fractures.

Ostseointegration has been largely undertaken overseas, but some patients have been followed up by the NHS. It has been reported that the first NHS osseointergration surgery took place in England at the end of 2022. We don't know what will happen going forwards and whether osseointegration will be offered on the NHS, but if it is, it is likely that strict criteria will be applied to qualifying participants.

Osseointegration is available for above knee and below knee amputees but there is a higher risk of complications with trans-tibial bone anchors hence it is much less common for below knee amputees. If a Claimant decides that osseointegration is for them, ensure they have obtained proper advice about the different options for surgery.

Neural Interfaces

Neural interfaces can include brain-computer interfaces and peripheral nerve interfaces. The former can provide a direct link between the user's brain and the prosthetic limb enabling them to control their movements through their thoughts. Peripheral nerve interfaces connect the prosthetic limb to the peripheral nerves allowing the user to experience sensations such as touch and temperature.

Neural interfaces can improve a user's control, co-ordination and their experience of the limb.

Cosmesis

A cosmesis is used for cosmetic purposes and can help with maintaining the psychological wellbeing of Claimants, providing them with a visually appealing and lifelike prosthesis.

There have been advancements in the materials and techniques used to produce cosmesis which means that limbs can mimic the shape, texture and colour of the original limb. Cosmesis can be vital to the overall rehabilitation and quality of life for Claimants.

It is worth considering whether a Claimant may benefit from a cosmesis, even where they do not consider they will use a functional prosthesis.

Roliner material

There have also been advancements in the materials used such as Roliner which has been in development for eight years. Badly fitting prosthetics can have a significant impact on a Claimant's life; roliner material allows an amputee to change the shape, volume, and stiffness of the liner that is used to connect a prosthetic limb's socket to a residual leg.

Pursuing these new developments is expensive, however the law is clear; the Claimant is entitled to be put in the position that they would otherwise have been in had the negligence not occurred.

It is important to remember that when there is consideration of any prosthetic provision, it is for the Claimant and their treating clinician to decide whether or not such provision is appropriate. Any treating recommendations should be supported by the experts. This is particularly important as the availability of cutting-edge technology increases.

There also needs to be proper and thorough investigation of the provision along with the necessity for any appropriate surgical or other procedures and rehabilitation input.

Recoverability

As above, prosthetics have become multifunctional. They are lighter and easier to operate; however, this comes at a considerable cost. More advanced prosthetics are not available on the NHS. The question then arises to what extent will a court allow recoverability of the more advanced prosthetic.

This very issue was explored in the case of Miller -v- Imperial College NHS Healthcare NHS Trust [2014] EWHC 3772 (QB).

The Claimant, aged 63 at the time, underwent a below and then above knee amputation following negligent treatment by the Defendant. Liability was admitted and therefore, only the issue of quantum remained in dispute.

One area of contention between the parties was the cost of a more advanced prosthetic leg.

Upon trialling a computerised 'C Leg' prosthetic, the Claimant quickly experienced notable improvements. She found it significantly lighter and more stable, which enhanced her mobility and eliminated the falls she had previously suffered with other prosthetics.

The hospital applied for funding to provide it to her, but that was refused by the Primary Care Trust ("PCT"). The cost of a C-Leg was £28,000. The Claimant therefore went back to using the 'SK2 free knee and foot' ("SK2") prosthetic which she was using previously. The SK2 was the lightest and best option in terms of a free knee and foot, but she still had "*all sorts of problems with it.*"

When the Claimant prepared her first witness statement, she had just been made aware that there was a more advanced prosthetic available, called the Genium prosthetic. She requested to trial the prosthetic "...

as it is safer and more stable". She had been advised that the Genium prosthetic would provide much more stability.

Both parties' care experts agreed that the Genium prosthetic improved the Claimant's mobility and gait and would reduce her risk of falling which in turn would improve her confidence.

A few weeks prior to trial the Claimant provided the court with DVD evidence of her trialling two prosthetic legs – the more expensive Genium argued for by the Claimant and the Orion as contented by the Defendant. The DVD evidence showed her undertaking a range of activities using both prosthetics.

The Judge said:

> *"In summary, the DVD in my judgment demonstrated that in every respect in which a test was performed the Genium was significantly more effective than the Orion in terms of restoring the mobility and confidence which the Claimant would have had before the accident. Neither limb, of course, is in anyway a substitute for the lost leg...The level of mobility, confidence, and gait, and, most importantly, stamina in being able to walk any distance, is far reduced with both. It seemed to me that the evidence of the DVD was that the Genium is, to a significant degree, the product best suited to cater for Mrs Miller's needs. It is nevertheless necessary to consider the medical experts' views before reaching a conclusion."*

The Judge was guided by the approach at paragraph 94 in the judgment of Lloyd Jones J, as he then was, in *A v Powys Health Board [2007] EWHC 2996*:

> *"The basis of assessment is the test of reasonableness as stated in Rialis v Mitchell, (Court of Appeal, 6th July 1984) and*

> *Sowden v Lodge [2005] 1 WLR 2129. The Claimant is entitled to damages to meet her reasonable requirements and reasonable needs arising from her injuries. In deciding what is reasonable it is necessary to consider first whether the provision chosen and claimed is reasonable and not whether, objectively, it is reasonable or whether other provision would be reasonable. Accordingly, if the treatment claimed by the Claimant is reasonable it is no answer for the defendant to point to cheaper treatment which is also reasonable. Rialis and Sowden were concerned with the appropriate care regime. However, the principles stated in those cases apply equally to the assessment of damages in respect of aids and equipment. In determining what is required to meet the Claimant's reasonable needs it is necessary to make findings as to the nature and extent of the Claimant's needs and then to consider whether what is proposed by the Claimant is reasonable having regard to those needs. (Massey v Tameside and Glossop Acute Services NHS Trust [2007] EWHC 317 (QB), per Teare J. at para. 59; Taylor v Chesworth and MIB [2007] EWHC 1001 (QB), per Ramsay J. at para 84.)"*

The Court allowed the more expensive prosthetic in Miller -v- Imperial College NHS Healthcare NHS Trust; the Claimant was entitled to damages to meet her reasonable needs arising from her injuries.

In Miller, the Judge ruled in favour of the Claimant receiving a more advanced prosthesis, determining that she was entitled to one that more closely restored her to the position she would have been in had the amputation not occurred.

The key to the Claimant's success in her recoverability of the sophisticated limb was the evidence she was able to produce in support. If acting for the Claimant, it is essential to ensure that any claim for any prosthetic is supported by the medico legal experts and treating clinicians, and if an interim payment is received, it is important to use this to trial a prosthetic if possible, so that persuasive evidence can be submitted in support of the claim.

Practical tips

When considering a claim for prosthetics, the following points should be considered:

- Being unrealistic about prosthetic needs – the Claimant needs to show an intention to purchase and use the prosthesis.
- The prosthetic should be trialled with the purpose and the benefit evidenced clearly.
- Where a prosthetic is trialled, videos of the prosthetic being trialled should be obtained.

It is important to note that there are limited provisions available on the NHS. Practitioners need to consider not only the provisions which are available on the NHS but those that can be accessed privately. Practitioners must also ensure that the case manager is aware of the range of prosthetics available and the advancements in technology. They must understand the Claimant's lifestyle and goals and work closely with the prosthetist to ensure the prosthetic is tailored to the Claimant. Choosing the correct prosthesis is vital to enabling Claimant to attain more independence, functionality and improve their quality of life.

References

1. National Institutes of Health (NIH) (n.d.) *NIH 3D: Prosthetics Collection.* NIH. Available at: https://3d.nih.gov/collections/prosthetics?tab=search

2. MedlinePlus Magazine / National Institutes of Health (NIH) (2023) *Prosthetics through the ages.* NIH MedlinePlus Magazine. Available at: https://magazine.medlineplus.gov/article/prosthetics-through-the-ages

3. MCOP (Medical Center Orthotics & Prosthetics) (n.d.) *Osseointegration Prosthetics: The Complete Guide to Osseointegrated Prosthetics for Amputees.* MCOP. Available at: https://mcopro.com/blog/resources/osseointegration-prosthetics-for-amputees/

4. Bush & Co (n.d.) *Revolutionary advancements in prosthetics: Overcoming limitations and restoring abilities.* Bush & Co. Available at: https://www.bushco.co.uk/news/latest-tech-in-prosthetics-and-what-it-does.html

5. Imperial College London (2025) *New material allows amputees to adjust fit of prosthetic limbs throughout day.* Imperial College London. Available at: https://www.imperial.ac.uk/news/262153/new-material-allows-amputees-adjust-prosthetic/

6. Keoghs LLP (2023) *NHS Osseointegration: A step forward for amputees?* Keoghs Insight. Available at: https://keoghs.co.uk/keoghs-insight/nhs-osseointegration-a-step-forward-for-amputees

7. Osseointegration.org (n.d.) *Osseointegration: Research and Clinical Evidence.* Osseointegration.org. Available at:

https://osseointegration.org/osseointegration-research-clinical-evidence/

8. Weightmans LLP (2025) *Strengthening amputation rehabilitation and prosthetic services: New NHS England guidance (May 2025)*. Weightmans LLP. Available at: https://www.weightmans.com/media-centre/news/strengthening-amputation-rehabilitation-and-prosthetic-services-new-nhs-england-guidance-may-2025/

9. Lexology (2023) *Osseointegration available on the NHS.* Lexology. Available at: https://www.lexology.com/library/detail.aspx?g=2942b586-88ca-4b31-bd48-39837a46cc64

CHAPTER NINE

PRACTICAL CONSIDERATIONS FOR SETTLEMENT

Before settling an amputation claim, there are a number of practical considerations to take into account to ensure fair compensation. It is important to remember that where the Claimant is a Protected Party or a child, settlement (and any interim payment) will always need the approval of the Court.

Compensation Recovery Unit (CRU)

It is vital that the CRU position is checked before making or accepting an offer of settlement. If the CRU certificate has expired, then an up-to-date certificate must be obtained. The certificate will set out the amount of recoverable benefits that must be repaid to the Department for Work and Pensions from the compensation. A failure to obtain the most up-to-date position regarding CRU can lead to complications to settlements.

As per CPR 36.20 a defendant who makes a Part 36 offer must state either whether the offer is made without regard to any reliability for recoverable amounts or that it is intended to include any deductible amount. The rules also state that before making the Part 36 offer, the offeror must apply for a certificate. The offeror's Part 36 offer must state:-

1. The gross amount of compensation;

2. The name and amount of any deductible amounts by which the gross amount is reduced; and,

3. The net amount of compensation.

If a CRU certificate is applied for, but has not been received at the time that an offer is made then the offer must be clarified by providing the information above no later than seven days after receipt of the certificates.

It is crucial that the CRU position is confirmed so that this settlement award accurately reflects the net award to be made to the claimant after deduction of recoverable benefits.

It is also important to ensure that the CRU certificate is correct and if it is not then the certificate should be appealed. A CRU certificate can only be appealed after the claim has concluded and all monies due to the CRU have been paid. The first step is to request a mandatory reconsideration, which must be done within one month of paying the money. If the outcome of the mandatory reconsideration is not satisfactory then an appeal can be lodged. This must be done within one month from the date the mandatory reconsideration notice was sent. The grounds for appealing can include incorrect amounts or rates specified in the certificate, or if the benefits listed were not related to the accident, injury or disease. The process involves submitting a written notice to HMCTS and the appeal will be heard by an appeals tribunal.

Periodical payments

A periodical payment award can be beneficial for both Claimants and Defendants. It is important to consider whether a periodical payment award is an appropriate method for compensating long-term needs.

Periodical payments offer security to a Claimant as they ensure the Claimant has sufficient funds to cover their ongoing needs such as care and case management. Claimants are guaranteed to receive tax-free payments for the rest of their life which are indexed to mitigate the effects of litigation. However, awards cannot be changed if a Claimant's needs change or if they require significant capital expenditure and therefore, they are inflexible.

For defendants, periodical payments can avoid overcompensating a claimant. They are particularly effective where life-expectancy is uncertain, because they end upon a Claimant's death. Practically, periodical payments means that the costs of usually very high care claims can be spread out over years which relieves the financial pressure on Defendants. In terms of disadvantages, the market can fluctuate and a defendant will be keen to ensure payments are secure and are adequately indexed to reflect inflation and wage growth.

Financial advice should be sought to ensure periodical payments are the most suitable award. If settlement requires approval, the Court will have to be satisfied that it is an appropriate method of settlement and will often refer to the financial planner's recommendations.

The Court will need to carefully consider whether a periodical payment order is appropriate, and in doing so must have regard to the Claimant's needs and preferences. They will consider the following:-

1. The Claimant's preferred form of award;

2. The nature of financial advice received; and,

3. The scale of annual payments.

The Court must also be satisfied that the continuity of payment under the order is reasonably secure.

PI Trusts

Where a claimant is receiving means tested benefits, then it is important to explain to them that their eligibility to continue receiving such benefits may be impacted by the compensation award and they should consider opening a personal injury trust into which their compensation can be paid. The benefit of opening a trust will mean that the compensation is ring fenced and will not be taken into account for means tested assessments. Claimants should be advised to seek appropriate advice around opening a Trust.

Where compensation is already being paid into a deputyship account on behalf of an adult Claimant receiving means-tested benefits then it is not necessary to open a separate trust, if that compensation is their only means of income. However, if income is being received via other means this will need to be considered carefully as a second trust may be needed.

If a Claimant wishes to invest their award, they should obtain specialist advice.

Provisional damages (CPR 41)

Earlier in this guide, we have considered the complications that may arise from amputations, and it is important to consider whether a Claimant's risk of deterioration or complication in the future is dealt with as part of the final settlement, or whether an order for provisional damages is appropriate. The latter is particularly beneficial where there are uncertainties around the Claimant's future condition. A provisional damages award can be beneficial for both parties. Such awards ensure that a Claimant is not under compensated if their condition deteriorates, and Defendants are also protected from over settling a case.

Where a Claimant is claiming provisional damages, the Particulars of Claim must include a statement that the Claimant is seeking an award for provisional damages and the grounds on which the award is being sought. The Court must be satisfied that Section 32A of the Senior Courts Act or Section 51 of the County Courts Act applies to the claim.

It is important to note that if an acknowledgement of service or defence is not filed in accordance with the relevant rules within the time specified, then a Claimant may not, unless he abandons his claim for provisional damages, enter judgment in default. In these circumstances, a Claimant should make an application in accordance with CPR Part 23 for directions. The Master or District Judge will usually direct for the following issues to be determine:-

1. Whether the claim is appropriate for a provisional damages award;

2. And if so, on what terms and to the amount of immediate damages.

The procedure for provisional damages is set out in CPR 41.

The process for applying for provisional damages is as follows:

1. At least 28 days written notice must be given by the Claimant to the Defendant of their intention to apply for further damages

2. If the address of the Defendant's insurers is known, then 28 days' written notice must also be given to the Defendant's insurers

3. Within 21 days thereafter, the Claimant must apply for directions.

It is therefore very important that where an order for provisional damages has been made, that the Claimant is aware of the time-limits.

If an Order is made for Provisional Damages, it is vital that it covers the following:

1. The disease or type of deterioration in respect of which the application is being made must be specified.

2. The order must specify the period within which such an application may be made.

3. Where an order is made in respect of more than one disease or deterioration, the order should cover each disease or deterioration and the time limits for bringing an application for the same.

4. The Court should direct what documentation should be preserved to support a future application for provisional damages.

The time limit for applying for provisional damages can be extended, but only one application for further damages can be made for each disease or type of deterioration specified.

In the case of *Whitcomb vJ Keith Park Solicitors [2023] EWCA Civ 326* the Claimant brought a claim against his solicitors for failing to advise him about provisional damages and failing to obtain a plastic surgeon's report.

The original claim arose from a road traffic accident in July 2002 where the claimant suffered severe leg and foot injuries as well as PTSD. The claimant settled his case in December 2009 for £150,000. The Claimant was advised there was a risk that he could be under settling his claim, should his condition deteriorate. However he was not advised about the possibility of provisional damages and incorrectly advised that a lump sum payment was the only option available to him. Unfortunately, his condition deteriorated and in January 2017 he was informed that he required a below the knee amputation. He contacted his original solicitors requesting the claim be revisited but was told this was not possible. He later brought a claim against his solicitors.

The court held that a failure to advise the Claimant on provisional damages was negligent. This case highlights the importance of advising Claimants of provisional damages and anticipating cases where future deterioration and chronic pain conditions should be considered.

In *Butler v Ministry of Justice [2015] EWHC 3384 (QB)*, the Claimant was 42 years old when he suffered an injury at work after slipping on some ice. He underwent numerous procedures and was in constant pain. The possibility of an elective amputation was discussed with his treating consultants.

Liability was agreed at 80% in the Claimant's favour. The main issue at the hearing related to quantum and whether provisional damages should be awarded.

Provisional damages are appropriate only where there is a real and measurable risk of a distinct future deterioration or complication.

> *"The principles and criteria to be applied are clear and can be expressed as follows: - (i) It is for the claimant to make an application for a provisional damages award. He is not obliged or required to do so. (ii) The Court may make such an award where it is admitted or proved that at some time in the future the claimant will, as a result of the defendant's act or omission which gave rise to the cause of action, develop some serious disease or suffer some serious deterioration in his physical or mental condition. (iii) CPR Rules 41.2 and 41.3 provide that if the claim for provisional damages is pleaded and the statutory criteria are fulfilled, then the Court nonetheless has the discretion as to whether or not to make a provisional award or whether in fact to make a final award. (iv) The order must specify the precise nature of the disease or deterioration which must occur before the claimant can seek a further determination and must specify whether the claimant may come back to the Court at any time during his or her life or if there is a time limit on such further application. (v) As set out in Kemp, therefore, the four stages can be summarised as a consideration: firstly as to whether or not the claimant has suffered personal injuries; secondly, whether or not he faces the chance or risk of; thirdly, developing a serious disease or deterioration in his condition; and fourthly, whether or not the Court should exercise the discretion.*

In Butler, the court refused provisional damages for the 25% risk of amputation because amputation was likely to improve symptoms. Medical evidence reported that amputation would give the Claimant approximately 70 percent improvement in his symptoms.

However, it allowed provisional damages for the 7.5% risk of serious complications **after** amputation (such as phantom limb pain or stump healing failure), as these represented a genuine risk of future worsening.

'The Electronic Communications Code: A Practical Guide – Second Edition' by Kerry Bretherton KC, James Castle, Mark Loveday
'A Practical Guide to the Independent School Standards – September 2023 Edition' by Sarah McKimm
'A Practical Guide to Estate Administration and Crypto Assets' by Richard Marshall
'A Practical Guide to Parental Alienation in Private and Public Law Children Cases' by Sam King QC & Frankie Shama
'Contested Heritage – Removing Art from Land and Historic Buildings' by Richard Harwood QC, Catherine Dobson, David Sawtell
'The Limits of Separate Legal Personality: When Those Running a Company Can Be Held Personally Liable for Losses Caused to Third Parties Outside of the Company' by Dr Mike Wilkinson
'A Practical Guide to Transgender Law' by Robin Moira White & Nicola Newbegin
'A Practical Guide to 'Stranded Spouses' in Family Law' by Mani Singh Basi
'A Practical Guide to Residential Freehold Conveyancing' by Lorraine Richardson
'A Practical Guide to Pensions on Divorce for Lawyers' by Bryan Scant
'A Practical Guide to Challenging Sham Marriage Allegations in Immigration Law' by Priya Solanki
'A Practical Guide to Digital Communications Evidence in Criminal Law' by Sam Willis
'A Practical Guide to Legal Rights in Scotland' by Sarah-Jane Macdonald
'A Practical Guide to New Build Conveyancing' by Paul Sams & Rebecca East
'A Practical Guide to Inherited Wealth on Divorce' by Hayley Trim
'A Practical Guide to Practice Direction 12J and Domestic Abuse in Private Law Children Proceedings' by Rebecca Cross & Malvika Jaganmohan
'A Practical Guide to Confiscation and Restraint' by Narita Bahra QC, John Carl Townsend, David Winch
'A Practical Guide to the Law of Forests in Scotland' by Philip Buchan
'A Practical Guide to Health and Medical Cases in Immigration Law' by Rebecca Chapman & Miranda Butler
'A Practical Guide to Bad Character Evidence for Criminal Practitioners by Aparna Rao
'A Practical Guide to Extradition Law post-Brexit' by Myles Grandison et al
'A Practical Guide to Hoarding and Mental Health for Housing Lawyers' by Rachel Coyle

'Stephens on Contractual Indemnities' by Richard Stephens
'A Practical Guide to the EU Succession Regulation' by Richard Frimston
'A Practical Guide to Solicitor and Client Costs – Second Edition' by Robin Dunne
'Constructive Dismissal – Practice Pointers and Principles' by Benjimin Burgher
'A Practical Guide to Religion and Belief Discrimination Claims in the Workplace' by Kashif Ali
'A Practical Guide to the Law of Medical Treatment Decisions' by Ben Troke
'Fundamental Dishonesty and QOCS in Personal Injury Proceedings: Law and Practice' by Jake Rowley
'A Practical Guide to the Law in Relation to School Exclusions' by Charlotte Hadfield & Alice de Coverley
'A Practical Guide to Divorce for the Silver Separators' by Karin Walker
'The Right to be Forgotten – The Law and Practical Issues' by Melissa Stock
'A Practical Guide to Planning Law and Rights of Way in National Parks, the Broads and AONBs' by James Maurici QC, James Neill et al
'A Practical Guide to Election Law' by Tom Tabori
'A Practical Guide to the Law in Relation to Surrogacy' by Andrew Powell
'A Practical Guide to Claims Arising from Fatal Accidents – Second Edition' by James Patience
'A Practical Guide to Asbestos Claims' by Jonathan Owen & Gareth McAloon
'A Practical Guide to Stamp Duty Land Tax in England and Northern Ireland' by Suzanne O'Hara
'A Practical Guide to the Law of Farming Partnerships' by Philip Whitcomb
'A Practical Guide to the Law of Unlawful Eviction and Harassment – Second Edition' by Stephanie Lovegrove
'A Practical Guide to Costs in Personal Injury Claims – Second Edition' by Matthew Hoe
'A Practical Guide to the General Data Protection Regulation (GDPR) – Second Edition' by Keith Markham
'A Practical Guide to Working with Litigants in Person and McKenzie Friends in Family Cases' by Stuart Barlow
'Protecting Unregistered Brands: A Practical Guide to the Law of Passing Off' by Lorna Brazell
'A Practical Guide to Secondary Liability and Joint Enterprise Post-Jogee' by Joanne Cecil & James Mehigan

'A Practical Guide to the Pre-Action RTA Claims Protocol for Personal Injury Lawyers' by Antonia Ford

'A Practical Guide to Neighbour Disputes and the Law' by Alexander Walsh

'A Practical Guide to Coercive Control for Legal Practitioners and Victims' by Rachel Horman

'A Practical Guide to the Law of Driverless Cars – Second Edition'

by Alex Glassbrook, Emma Northey & Scarlett Milligan

'A Practical Guide to TOLATA Claims' by Greg Williams

'A Practical Guide to Elderly Law – Second Edition' by Justin Patten

'A Practical Guide to Responding to Housing Disrepair and Unfitness Claims' by Iain Wightwick

'A Practical Guide to the Law of Bullying and Harassment in the Workplace' by Philip Hyland

'How to Be a Freelance Solicitor: A Practical Guide to the SRA-Regulated Freelance Solicitor Model' by Paul Bennett

'A Practical Guide to Prison Injury Claims' by Malcolm Johnson

'A Practical Guide to Advising Clients at the Police Station' by Colin Stephen McKeown-Beaumont

'A Practical Guide to Antisocial Behaviour Injunctions – Second Edition' by Iain Wightwick

'Practical Mediation: A Guide for Mediators, Advocates, Advisers, Lawyers, and Students in Civil, Commercial, Business, Property, Workplace, and Employment Cases' by Jonathan Dingle with John Sephton

'The Mini-Pupillage Workbook' by David Boyle

'A Practical Guide to Crofting Law' by Brian Inkster

'A Practical Guide to the Law of Domain Names and Cybersquatting' by Andrew Clemson

'A Practical Guide to the Law of Gender Pay Gap Reporting' by Harini Iyengar

'NHS Whistleblowing and the Law' by Joseph England

'Employment Law and the Gig Economy' by Nigel Mackay & Annie Powell

'A Practical Guide to Noise Induced Hearing Loss (NIHL) Claims' by Andrew Mckie, Ian Skeate, Gareth McAloon

'An Introduction to Beauty Negligence Claims – A Practical Guide for the Personal Injury Practitioner' by Greg Almond

'Intercompany Agreements for Transfer Pricing Compliance' by Paul Sutton

'Zen and the Art of Mediation' by Martin Plowman

'A Practical Guide to Adoption for Family Lawyers' by Graham Pegg

www.ingramcontent.com/pod-product-compliance
Lightning Source LLC
LaVergne TN
LVHW022312200926
848481LV00004B/1306
9781918241105